ChooseLife!

YOUR GUIDE TO PROSPERITY IN YOUR SPIRIT, SOUL AND BODY.

BY
SOPHIA E. HAYNES, ESQ.

Copyright @2020 Sophia E. Haynes All Rights Reserved

No part of this publication may be reproduced, stored in a retrieval system, or transmitted in any form or by any means, electronic, mechanical, photocopying, recording, scanning, or otherwise, without the prior written permission of the author.

Design, Layout and Cover Design
Pixel Studio

ISBN:

Ebook-978-1-7361372-0-8
Print-978-1-7361372-1-5

Library of Congress Control Number:

2020923595

SEH Enterprises, LLC

sehenterprises@outlook.com

DEDICATION

This book is dedicated to my maternal grandfather, James Lee Conner. We called him "Paw". His unconditional love and support gave me the courage to step out and pursue my purpose.

CONTENTS

Chapter 1: Every change begins with a decision. *1*

Chapter 2: It is what I say it is: The Power of Confession. *5*

Chapter 3: Embrace Wellness. *9*

    Spiritual *9*

    Physical *10*

    How is your oral health? *10*

    Rest to Reset. *11*

    You are what you eat. *12*

    30 minutes a day keeps just about everything away. *13*

    Intellectual *13*

Chapter 4: Don't manage stress, eliminate it. *15*

    Don't mess with the cuteness. *16*

Chapter 5: Consistency is the key to the breakthrough. *19*

What I Know For Sure. *23*

More about ChooseLife! *25*

"It always seems impossible until it is done."

— Nelson Mandela

WHAT THIS BOOK IS AND WHAT IT IS NOT...

This book was written for everyday folks—single and married, kids and no kids, old and young. It is my story of how I have incorporated a common-sense approach for the last two decades to live in peace as I prepare to live long and finish strong.

In my almost half century of life, I have not had any illnesses nor do I take any medications. A major key to that is I follow a mantra encapsulated within a quote from Mahatma Gandhi that says, "*I will not let anyone walk through my mind with their dirty feet.*" That is the decision I made many years ago and it was life changing.

This book is not the latest fitness craze, diet, or life plan. I am not a fitness trainer, therapist or life coach. I am your quintessential "Auntie" whose purpose is to inspire you to pursue the greatness which lies within your purpose. It is my desire to share what has helped me to stay at peace and well despite the same challenges that every other human being faces in our world. I was raised in humble beginnings and had to figure out many things on my own as I blazed my own trail. From those humble beginnings, I have worked hard and rose to senior levels in government service, but not without conflict and hard times. I have not arrived, but continue to press because as Pastor A.R. Bernard once said "purpose is not static, it is dynamic."

I have learned that this world is chaotic, but it does not have to consume you. I made the decision to ChooseLife! and you can too. What you read here will not be anything new or earth shaking. We have more information at our finger tips now than at any other time in history. It is the execution that we lack. The power in these principles lies within their simplicity. It is my hope that as you experience this book, it will stir you to develop your own individual action plan for a more peaceful and productive life on purpose.

CHAPTER 1: EVERY CHANGE BEGINS WITH A DECISION.

Decisions are the hardest thing to make especially when it is a choice between where you should be and where you want to be.
Unknown

Life is a series of decisions. You awake in the morning and decide if and when you will get out of bed. You decide each day if you will bathe (hopefully that is in the affirmative), what you will wear, breakfast or no breakfast etc. Nothing happens without a decision made by you. Even no decision is a decision. Where you are now is a culmination of the decisions that you have made in your past. What your life looks like in the future will be the result of the decisions you make now. Are you presently where you thought you would be at this stage of your life? If not, look back to determine what decision(s) you made that became the turning point to take you off course and simply make a better decision.

It has been said that every decision is an open door to reality. What I have learned is every decision has built in consequences. When you make the decision, you choose the consequences—good, bad or otherwise. Therefore, your decisions are extremely important. One of my favorite bible verses in this area is Deuteronomy 30:19 in the New Living Translation. It says: "Today I have given you the choice between life and death, between blessings and curses. Now I call on heaven and earth to witness the choice you make. Oh, that you would choose life, so that you and your descendants might live!" This verse was very illuminating for me because when something happens of my own doing, I simply review the choice that heaven and earth witnessed that I made regardless of the reason why I did so. Knowing this places me in charge of my destiny, regardless of what may have happened or not in my past or currently happening in my present.

ChooseLife! requires you to evaluate all of the areas of your life and make a conscious decision to discard anything that does not breed life into your being. For me this includes my perspective about the occurrences that happen in life that are out of my control, what I eat, how much sleep I give to my body, what I see, what I hear, and who or what I choose to engage. What I have learned is what you see and hear eventually finds its way into your heart and out of the abundance of the heart your mouth will speak. I always want my words to speak life.

I also made the decision to not "take" offense at anything. What I discovered is just because someone gives offense does not mean that I have to take or receive it. I made the decision to allow them to hold on to their offense because offense and its effects do not breed life into my body. Moreover, it is not healthy to allow anyone to have control over you and your emotions by their words and/or actions. I encourage you to take a moment to make the decision to ChooseLife! in every area, and to make a plan to bring that decision into fruition.

ChooseLife! Execution Points:

- Take the time to reflect upon what drives your decisions.
- Make the decision to reject anything (words, thoughts, actions etc.) that does not produce life.

My ChooseLife! Action Plan:

CHAPTER 2: IT IS WHAT I SAY IT IS: THE POWER OF CONFESSION

The power to tear down or build up lies in your tongue.
Unknown

My mother and my father made the decision to name me Sophia. I learned in my early twenties that the name Sophia is of Greek origin and means wisdom. So every time they refer to or call upon me, they confess that I AM wisdom. What are you confessing over your children? Have they started to manifest what you call them either by name or what you say about them in general? What have you been saying about yourself?

The reality is words have power, and tomorrow you will have to live with the things you say today. Why? Because if you say something long enough, you begin to believe it. What you truly believe, your heart will devise a way to bring it to pass in your life. What have you been saying about your life, your family, and your career objectives? Make no mistake about it you will have what you say. With this revelation, I developed a practice that helps me to be conscious of the words that I speak. This means when I say things that I do not want to see manifested in my life, I immediately correct myself and say out loud what I truly want.

To further assist myself in this area, I also cultivated over the years what I call the 3 second rule. I use the same when preparing my clients for trial. How the 3 second rule works is if a statement is made or question presented, I wait 3 seconds before I respond. In this way, I make sure that I heard and understood the question or statement. If I did not understand, then I ask for clarification prior to responding.

I had to do so because I discovered in conversation that I was not an active listener. Like most, I participated in conversations to hear enough to react because I was focused more on defending myself instead of truly listening. Active listening requires one to stay engaged with your conversation partner in a positive way. As a result, you listen attentively while someone else speaks, paraphrasing and reflecting back what is said, while withholding judgment and advice. Although I am still perfecting this art, especially in matters that I am passionate about, I recognize that it is extremely beneficial in making sure that I say only what I want to see in my life.

ChooseLife! Execution Points

- Make positive affirmations daily over you, your family and all those connected to you.
- Say only what you want to see manifested in your life.

My ChooseLife! Action Plan:

CHAPTER 3: EMBRACE WELLNESS

The first wealth is health.
Ralph Waldo Emerson

Wellness is defined as the quality or state of being healthy in body and mind, especially as the result of deliberate effort. Another view of wellness is approaching one's health from a point of view that emphasizes preventing illness and prolonging life, as opposed to emphasizing treating diseases. I believe that we all are spirit beings who have a soul and live in a physical body. Our soul is made up of our mind, will and emotions. It is important that each component of our being is well to live fully and pursue purpose. The radical truth is what you display outwardly is often a manifestation of what is happening internally.

SPIRITUAL

My belief in God has grounded me. Times of prayer and meditation remind me to maintain a standard, keep my heart pure, and treat others how I would like to be treated. Do I get it right all the time? Absolutely not. However, knowing that I am loved and forgiven gives me the strength to regroup, learn the lesson and press forward. With this foundation, I approach challenges in life not with the thought of why is this happening to me, but what is this designed to teach me?

I begin each day with prayer and meditation. This has resulted in my ability to respond to issues as they arise and not simply react. Because I ultimately work hard to keep my heart pure, I endeavor to always do what's right because it is right and then do it right. I remain at peace because I know everything eventually works itself out for my good.

PHYSICAL

We are given one temple to experience this thing we call life. I must confess that I have not always treated my temple well. Society has taught us to wear "busy" as a badge without actually being fully present for any of it. Unfortunately, working hard does not necessarily mean that you are working smart. We push and push and eventually the toll begins to show. This could take on the form of depression, anxiety, high blood pressure, diabetes, obesity, and other chronic diseases which are either caused or exacerbated by stress.

HOW IS YOUR ORAL HEALTH?

Like most, my dental insurance covers at least 2 dental cleanings per year. During one of my visits, my provider informed me of the connection between my oral health and overall wellness. I performed a little research and found that the Journal of the American Dental Association advised that your oral health can show signs that reveal nutritional deficiencies or general infection. Chronic and systemic diseases like diabetes, for example may first become apparent because of mouth lesions or other oral problems. They specifically noted:

"The mouth is filled with countless bacteria, some linked to tooth decay and periodontal (gum) disease. Researchers have found that periodontitis (the advanced form of periodontal disease that can cause tooth loss) is linked with other health problems, such as cardiovascular disease, stroke and bacterial pneumonia. Likewise, pregnant women with periodontitis may be at increased risk of delivering preterm and/or low-birth-weight infants[1]."

REST TO RESET.

The reality is our bodies need times of genuine rest. I have committed to 8 hours of sleep each night and have found that it is a huge factor in how I avoid stress during the day. During times of rest, your body heals itself and prepares to function as designed. I am often asked how do you sleep 8 hours? I had to first acknowledge that just because you are sleeping does not necessarily mean that you are resting. I have actually slept 8 hours because my body is trained to do so, but woke up tired. What was my solution? A solid nighttime ritual. Because your body will do whatever you train it to do, my nighttime ritual was designed to train my body when it was time to rest. I also incorporate reading under my intellectual wellness routine as part of my regular nighttime ritual. More importantly for me, I removed the television from my bedroom and hung blackout curtains. In this way, my body is trained that once I get in the bed, it is time to go to sleep.

Another important investment in my sound sleep is high thread count sheets and a great pillow. You would be surprised what a difference it makes. This sequence of events, removes the clutter from my mind so that my mind is not racing and I can actually rest. This particular ritual may not work for you, but I encourage you to find what does work for you. It will make a world of difference in how you feel upon rising each day.

The 2020 pandemic taught us that we do not *have to* be anywhere. It caused us to sit down and really concentrate on what was important. I gave myself permission to take one full day out of the week and just rest. I incorporated one of my favorite treats, a spa day. Before the pandemic, I would treat myself once or twice a year to a luxurious day spa. I called it my "reset". I would spend a few days getting pampered and rested and then go right back to being "busy" all over again. It was a vicious cycle. The pandemic challenged me to question myself as to why my spa experience that brought me so much peace and rest

---

1   JADA, Vol. 137 April 2006

was not a part of my regular routine. Quite frankly, I did not have an answer. So Self-Care Sunday was born!

During Self-Care Sunday, I pamper myself for at least an hour each week with my "temple maintenance treats". Don't we all deserve one hour? I have a bubble bath, facial treatment, hand treatment and foot treatment—all while Pandora entertains me and aromatherapy candles soothe my senses. The result is a reset each week which allows me to be more productive. What is your reset?

YOU ARE WHAT YOU EAT.

Being raised in the South, southern hospitality is a staple. This includes every form of fried food and baked good. You certainly cannot allow a guest to leave without feeding them or offering something refreshing to drink. A true southerner does not tolerate food without rich taste. The problem is our source of flavor is not always the best for us physically. Consequently, we then begin to see all of the physical ailments that our parents and grandparents experienced in our bodies because we made the same choices.

I took some time several years ago to really pray about what was best for my body. I was led to begin a plant-based diet. I also had to accept that my body was 70% water, so pure water had to become a part of my routine. It took me a while to fully incorporate it all—old habits die hard. I am now so glad that I did. I have found that the preventive works best for me. I am not saying that you should adopt exactly the same, but I suggest that you take your health in your hands, and figure out what works best for you.

To get started, I invested in myself by taking a series of tests to find out where I stood with my vitamin and mineral levels, thyroid function and food sensitivities. I learned that many foods that are normally regarded as healthy in general had an inflammatory response in MY body. For example, I found out that I should avoid grapes, peaches and strawberries. I also learned that adequate rest was vitally important for my blood type. No matter how well we eat, we will never consume all the vitamins and minerals we need each day from our eating plans. Consequently, proper supplements became a staple in my routine—vitamins, minerals and omegas. I noticed a major difference in how I felt when I was not consistent with my supplements.

30 MINUTES A DAY KEEPS JUST ABOUT EVERYTHING AWAY.

Our bodies were designed to move. The choice to complete 30 minutes of physical activity each day made a world of difference for me. My elliptical became my friend. The result was better sleep, release of stress response and balanced function in my body. Like my vitamin supplement intake, when I missed this investment in my health I could immediately tell the difference. I have found that I do not need to live in the gym to live optimally, but my body does need to move.

Likewise, your body needs to move also. There are an abundance of free options. Many municipalities have developed walking trails. Local parks and community centers with tracks are also an option, and let's not forget what has become known as You Tube University. I remember as a kid growing up that many would go to the malls before they opened and would simply walk. Most smart phones have an app that will record your steps. Another great option is the wellness programs through your employer or your health insurance. Many have free classes that you can sign up for. Will you make the commitment to move for better health?

INTELLECTUAL

Intellectual Wellness is the ability to be open to new ideas, be creative, think critically and seek out new challenges. It makes one well rounded and in a continual posture of growth. At this point in your life, are you taking the time to learn and read? Are you pursuing things that challenge you and develop your mind? When was the last time you read a good book, learned a new skill or allowed yourself to have a new experience? Intellectual Wellness is just as important as all of the other elements of wellness and is vital to wholeness. It keeps one focused and more adept at the other types of wellness.

ChooseLife! Execution Points:

- Rediscover a physical activity that you enjoy to ensure 30 minutes of movement each day.

- Purchase a 16 ounce water bottle and drink 16 ounces of water each time the clock strikes 12 until you drink at least a half a gallon of water each day.

My ChooseLife! Action Plan:

CHAPTER 4: DON'T MANAGE STRESS, ELIMINATE IT.

Between stimulus and response, one has the freedom to choose.
Stephen Covey

There has never been a truer statement than "if it costs you your peace, it is too expensive." Stress will kill you! It has been my experience that as long as you are walking in your purpose and keeping your heart pure, everything will fall into place. The last two years would have broken me if I did not have this revelation. I know that my purpose is to pursue justice. As test after test came, I chose to rest in what I knew and it all worked out every time. Truth always prevails.

I rest because I learned as a young prosecutor that none of my success was based upon my education or how much I prepared, even though those things are vital. I prosecuted a possession of marijuana case once. I put my best case forward, but it was a matter of knowing a truth without necessarily having all of the evidence that you would like to have to prove it. The jury returned a guilty verdict that completely surprised me. I remember asking within myself how and heard "this has nothing to do with you, you are simply the instrument". That was an ignited moment for me and from that point on I was free. The pressure was no longer on me. I simply had to yield.

A few years later, I had a similar experience when I argued a case before the Georgia Supreme Court. What happened at the lower court level was not just or fair. All seven justices agreed with me and a little girl who had been mauled by a pit bull received justice. This victory solidified this premise and was another ignited moment for me.

I now approach every assignment, personal and professional, with humility and in search of what my part is in the outcome that I believe has already been determined. I have found that you do not have to endure harmful stress, you can eliminate it. In simplest terms, stress is a natural, physical and mental reaction to life experiences either real or perceived. This means when life presents itself, you choose your response. When you know who you are, you are not moved by what you see you are anchored by what you know. As a part of my intellectual wellness, I study the habits of centenarians. One central practice for them all is they stay positive and do not allow themselves to worry about anything. If you have lived 100 years and I want to achieve the same or even more, I think that it would be wise for me to listen.

DON'T MESS WITH THE CUTENESS.

Your body was never designed to bear the weight of the negative. Carrying the cares of life causes stress. Chronic stress can suppress your immune system, upset your digestive system, increase your risk for heart attack and stroke, and speed up the aging process. So what are some of the causes of stress? One common area is what is known as keeping up with the _____. I will allow you to fill in the blank. One observes friends or family with the latest phones and gadgets and run out to obtain the same. The truth is most of the folks displaying the latest, greatest and shiniest do not own any of those items just the debt which keeps them from building true wealth.

I fell into a similar trap early in my career. As a practicing attorney, we are engrained with the thought of appearances. One such appearance is the "status car" typically a luxury line. It has become known as a symbol that one has reached a certain status in the profession. For me it was the Jaguar S-Type and then it was the Seven Series BMW. I came to love the creature comforts in each

CHAPTER 4: DON'T MANAGE STRESS, ELIMINATE IT.

vehicle—ride, heated seats, and speaker systems to name a few. Ironically, my inner cheapness prevailed and I went back to a Honda after each luxury vehicle. Guess what? When I maintained my Hondas, they rode as smoothly as the luxury cars. Additionally, the heated seats and sound systems in my Hondas worked equally as well. Go figure. Obviously, there is nothing wrong with driving luxury vehicles. I submit that you simply ask yourself why do you want it, what does it symbolize for you, and how does it fit into your plan for your life.

A few more stress inducing examples are facing big challenges, worry, and feeling out of control and overwhelmed by your responsibilities. Have you made decisions that are causing you stress? Does the big house or slick car actually hurt? What I have learned is I do not have to be a part of and know everything. More importantly, I choose to focus on where I am at the present time and to have impact there.

ChooseLife! Execution Points:

- Cultivate a deep breathing practice.
- Identify sources of stress and make a plan to eliminate them from your life.

My ChooseLife! Action Plan:

CHAPTER 5: CONSISTENCY IS THE KEY TO THE BREAKTHROUGH.

You will never find the time for anything. If you want time you must make it.

Charles Buxton

What are your habits and where did they come from? Believe it or not they came from the words that you have exposed yourself to and said. Words determine how you think. How you think determines how you feel. How you feel drives your decisions. Your decisions determine your actions. Your actions determine your habits. Your habits determine your character. Your character determines your destiny.

What are you planting consistently that is showing up in your life? How many times have you started and stopped initiatives, programs or activities that would benefit you? Time waits for no one. Years will pass without any action by you or whether you choose to engage or not. Wouldn't you rather look back and see that you have accomplished your goals? As we discussed earlier, it all starts with YOUR decision. ChooseLife! is not a fad, but a way of life that you must continually choose and live each day.

It has been said that it takes 21 days to form a new habit. If consistency has been an issue, I encourage you to break your goals down into daily and weekly increments until you cross the 21 day threshold. Often, setting long term permanent goals can become overwhelming if not planned properly. Don't defeat yourself before getting started. Life is a marathon and not a sprint. The joy comes from all of the great things that you learn on the journey and not necessarily in just making it to the destination.

ChooseLife! Execution Points:

- Create a list of goals and develop a daily practice toward reaching those goals.
- Set definite timelines toward the fulfillment of your goals.

My ChooseLife! Action Plan:

ChooseLife! Tip: Five hobbies (or one with all five components) outside of work that will help to construct an effective ChooseLife! plan

- One to generate income
- One to keep you in shape
- One that explores your creativity
- One to increase your knowledge
- One to ensure that your mindset continually evolves

Adapted from a post by Strati Georgopolus

WHAT I KNOW FOR SURE...

I can remember growing up watching Walter Cronkite on the CBS Evening News. He was a trusted news broadcaster because he simply provided the facts on the events of the day, and we were allowed to make up our own minds about how we thought about it. We are now not only bombarded with millions of images daily, but also commentary on those images. Unfortunately, as a society we are not the better for it. So much so many no longer know how to think critically for themselves.

Worrying about the comments and opinions of others personally, at work, and on social media has caused so many to pursue destructive habits. Sharing my experience here was not designed to instruct you on how to think or feel about anything. It was written to encourage you to make the decision to ChooseLife! and pursue your own ChooseLife! course of action.

After almost a half century of life, there are some key things that I know for sure. Love is the greatest force on the earth and against love there is no law. Love is a decision that has nothing to do with how I feel. Love for others begins with a healthy self-love. Self-love requires me to treat my mind and body well. Joy comes from what you know and not a feeling from a temporary moment. Finally, true success is discovering why you were born, embracing it, and walking it out for you are not in competition with anyone but yourself to become a better you each day.

No one can beat you at being authentically you. The way you look, think, your personality, and your life experiences were all designed to usher you into your destiny and the reason why you were born at the time you were born. Embrace it for someone is waiting on you and your gifts. #ChooseLife!

MORE ABOUT CHOOSELIFE!

ChooseLife! is the first installment of the *Life Series,* a trilogy of books designed to encourage the application of simple principles to live life well and without unnecessary complications. The idea for a book series on choosing life grew out of both life experience and all of the challenges the world faced in 2020. We all have a common desire to live our best life. We simply need a plan to do so, and the commitment to pursue. ChooseLife! is a global movement to help millions establish a foundation to enjoy life. It is our goal to reach one million people who will then influence their own one million until the world has made the life changing decision to #ChooseLife!

To contact us or get more information, please email us at YourLifeSeries@gmail.com or visit www.sophiaehaynes.com

Additional copies of this book in EBook and/or print formats are available through Amazon and all other major book retailers.

www.ingramcontent.com/pod-product-compliance
Lightning Source LLC
Chambersburg PA
CBHW062207100526
44589CB00014B/2000